2016 PRESIDENTIAL ELECTION GUIDE

Lori Cox Han
Chapman University

Diane J. Heith
St. John's University

D1247253

New York   Oxford
OXFORD UNIVERSITY PRESS

Oxford University Press is a department of the University of Oxford.
It furthers the University's objective of excellence in research,
scholarship, and education by publishing worldwide.

Oxford New York
Auckland Cape Town Dar es Salaam Hong Kong Karachi
Kuala Lumpur Madrid Melbourne Mexico City Nairobi
New Delhi Shanghai Taipei Toronto

With offices in
Argentina Austria Brazil Chile Czech Republic France Greece
Guatemala Hungary Italy Japan Poland Portugal Singapore
South Korea Switzerland Thailand Turkey Ukraine Vietnam

For titles covered by Section 112 of the US Higher Education Opportunity Act,
please visit www.oup.com/us/he for the latest information about pricing and
alternate formats.

Published by Oxford University Press
198 Madison Avenue, New York, New York 10016
http://www.oup.com

CIP Data is on file at the Library of Congress.

ISBN: 978-0-19-061052-4

Printing number: 9 8 7 6 5 4 3 2 1

Printed in the United States of America
on acid-free paper

Contents

PREFACE

Even in the age of the Internet, where we can instantly share viral cat videos, the only thing the United States really does together is vote for president. Although there are myriad state and local candidates on the ballot each election year, only the presidential choice is the same for every American at the polls on the first Tuesday in November. When you combine the fact that the presidential campaign is the only national race with the fact that many consider the office of the presidency the center of the political universe, it is no wonder the race draws such scrutiny. In *Presidents and the American Presidency*, we argue that "who chooses to run for president, and who succeeds in winning the election, greatly affects not only the day-to-day governing of the nation but the institution of the presidency as well" (Han and Heith 2013, p. 76).

The 2016 race exemplifies what the presidential campaign and election process has become: a four year, chaotic, media driven spectacle, where candidates draw intense attention and donors give outrageous sums of money. Unexpectedly, the pre-nomination phase revealed a high level of voter anger with politics as usual, as least on the Republican side. Donald Trump, real estate mogul and media entrepreneur, Carly Fiorina, former Hewlett Packard CEO, and Ben Carson, former Johns Hopkins pediatric neurosurgeon have reaped the benefits as outsiders in this period before voting even begins. On the Democratic side, the desire for difference has led to the unexpected rise of Vermont Senator Bernie Sanders. However, the juggernaut that has been the Hillary Clinton campaign during the pre-nomination phase makes the Sanders threat less serious than that posed by Trump and Carson for the traditional Republican candidates, Senator Marco Rubio (FL), former Florida Governor Jeb Bush, Ohio Governor John Kasich, and Senator Ted Cruz (TX).

In politics, the devil, as they say, is in the details. In the pages that follow, we explore the details that mattered in the pre-nomination phase and the details that will matter in the nomination period and in the general election. The pre-nomination phase was about money and endorsements. The primaries and caucus period, beginning February 3, are determined by the calendar, the rules, and turnout. The general election adds both phases together and rests on building a new coalition of nomination and general election voters.

We explore these details by being as timely as possible, placing the nitty-gritty of the 2016 race within current political science theory. We hope that by providing an understanding of what has happened, alongside a forecast driven by the behavior of candidates, parties, and voters, it will be possible to merge a textbook understanding of what matters in campaigns and elections with real-time events. We also hope a greater understanding of the process spurs participation, as without a wide swath of voter involvement the campaign and election of a president is not a reflection of national goals, values, wants, and needs. With voter involvement, the race for president can be so much more than narrow, elite battles for power and position.

ACKNOWLEDGMENTS

As we noted in *Presidents and the American Presidency*, neither of us would be presidency scholars who continue to be fascinated by leadership without the inspiration of our mentors, the late William W. Lammers of the University of Southern California and the late Elmer E. Cornwell, Jr. of Brown University. Their insight and theoretical understanding of the presidency and what surrounds it continue to be missed. The editorial team at Oxford University Press continues to support our efforts to explore the presidency from an archival and theoretical perspective, which we believe brings events into sharper focus. Although this look at 2016 is current and thus in flux, we employ the same approach to contextualizing behavior and explaining outcomes. Our friends and family continue to provide the love and support two professional women need to be successful. Ultimately, we created this book for our students— to give them a roadmap for watching, evaluating, and participating in the 2016 presidential election. We hope it spurs them to make their own voice heard. And finally—Taylor, Davis, and Owen—it is always for you.

Chapter 1

INTRODUCTION

Many nations have designed constitutions using the United States as a model, particularly with respect to their legislatures, the concepts of the separation of powers and the rule of law, voting-rights requirements, and many other aspects. Yet, no other country has copied the way Americans elect their presidents. Why is that? In general, American presidential elections are chaotic, complex, and cumbersome, which makes them difficult to understand and emulate. They are also long and expensive and rely on an institutional mechanism known as the Electoral College whose determination of the winner can often be at odds with the popular vote, a result that many other countries view as inequitable and illogical. Despite that American voters seem to dislike numerous aspects of presidential campaigns, specifically the role of money, media coverage, the length of the campaign, and a lack of substantive discussion about important policy issues, presidential campaigns are becoming even longer, more expensive, and subject to intense media coverage that is often vapid and superficial. Perhaps this is why voter turnout for presidential elections, while higher than that for any other type of election in the United States, is so low in comparison with other liberal democracies around the globe.

What does this mean for the 2016 presidential election? Leading up to the current presidential contest, the only thing that voters could count on was that, according to the 22nd Amendment to the Constitution, which limits presidents to two terms in office, President Barack Obama would not be on the ballot. However, no such mechanism exists to limit the duration of presidential campaigns. On November 6, 2012, Obama won a second term in office by defeating Republican nominee Mitt Romney.

1

Barack Obama (CSPAN)

Mitt Romney (AP Photo/Elise Amendola)

However, by the time Obama was sworn into office on January 20, 2013, American voters were already several weeks into the 2016 presidential campaign cycle. The reality of American presidential politics is that voters rarely get a break from the campaign process. Before anyone had a chance to recover from the onslaught of campaign ads, public opinion polls, news media coverage, and the endless predictions of outcomes of the presidential race, voters were immediately thrust into the next presidential campaign cycle, exposed to speculation about prospective candidates, potential frontrunners, and probable nominees and, ultimately, likely winners.

Whether they like it or not, American voters now live in a perpetual presidential campaign. The factors that contribute to this are a function of the nature of the political process and the structure of the primary campaign as defined by successive state-specific contests. First is the pre-nomination period, commonly referred to as the "invisible primary," during which numerous candidates jockey for viability—that is, earning name recognition and vying for early fundraising success, media coverage, and leads in public opinion polling, all in hope of laying the groundwork for success in the first voting contests. The second phase is the start of the nomination or primary season, which begins with the first two voting contests in Iowa and New Hampshire, followed by South Carolina and Nevada, and leading to numerous state primaries on what is called Super Tuesday. Several other states finish out the primary season with contests that run through June of the election year. Third, Democrats and Republicans then select their nominees, including their running mates, at their national conventions during the summer, to be followed by the unofficial start of the general election campaign on Labor Day. The entire process, which unofficially lasts for four years, culminates in the presidential election on the first Tuesday of November. To understand the politics, procedures, and processes during the upcoming 2016 presidential campaign, much can be learned by examining its evolution from its unofficial beginning in the closing days of the 2012 campaign cycle to its eventual finale on Election Day, November 8, 2016.

Chapter 2

THE PRE-NOMINATION PERIOD

Presidential campaigns have not always been so long and expensive, and campaign activities during the time before the first caucus/primary contests used to occur mostly behind closed doors. Journalist Arthur Hadley was the first to coin the term "invisible primary" in 1976 to reflect the fact that candidates customarily announced their campaigns only a few months before the Iowa Caucuses and New Hampshire Primary (the first contests since the early 1970s) and used the time before that to quietly seek support from prominent party members and donors.[1] Now, candidates announce their campaigns up to a year before the Iowa contest, and that has made activities during this period far from invisible. During this phase, presidential candidates are vetted by party officials and major financial backers, as well as the news media, as candidates attempt to showcase their viability for the general election. Two things matter more than anything else during this time—raising money and media coverage. Some now refer to the pre-nomination period as the "money primary," because raising campaign funds can say a lot about whether someone's campaign is for real. Money and media coverage also contribute to higher standing in early polls, which can be construed as candidate viability. A two-tiered campaign often emerges during these early months. A handful of candidates are considered viable early on, while others never break through to the top-tier of serious contenders (and as a result, do not receive much attention from the media or donors). As we discuss below, this has been a major feature of the early months of the 2016 presidential campaign for both the Democratic and Republican Parties.

The American news media, which loves to speculate and make predictions about future political outcomes, have also contributed greatly to the trend of extending the length of the pre-nomination phase. Media also contribute heavily to the vetting process, which determines a candidate's viability or lack thereof. The horse race coverage (as in, who's ahead, who's behind, who's winning, who's losing, etc.) that has dominated campaign coverage in recent decades has found a more permanent home as an everyday staple of political reporting, and the pre-nomination phase is no exception. Constant stories about candidates, their fundraising efforts, and their positions in the latest opinion polls focus on the game of politics and the personalities of the candidates as opposed to substantive discussions of policy alternatives. The lack of substance also leaves tremendous room for coverage that is superficial and negative in tone. Other consequences include longer campaigns that cost more money, evidenced by the fact that each successive presidential campaign in recent decades has set new fundraising and spending records. It's not surprising that many American voters feel apathetic and alienated by the political system and that voter turnout is low.

The Candidates: Republicans

Who emerged as the top-tier contenders during the summer and fall of 2015? The Republican field started out with 17 candidates but was winnowed to 15 in September 2015 with the early exits of former Texas Governor Rick Perry and Wisconsin Governor Scott Walker. Despite early momentum for both in terms of Super PAC funds and media buzz, neither was able to translate that into early polling success. Perry did not even make the cut among the top-ten Republican candidates (based on an aggregation of several polls) who participated in the first GOP debate on Fox News in August. (He instead participated in what many referred to as the "undercard" debate, which was televised earlier in the day and comprised mostly candidates who were at or below 1 percent in the polls). Walker, a second-term governor who also survived a recall effort in Wisconsin in 2012, ended his campaign on September 21 and urged other Republican candidates not likely to move up in the polls to do the same for the sake of the party. Walker's presidential campaign, which lasted just 70 days, was the shortest on record since 2000.[2]

Notable on the Republican side has been the support for and interest in antiestablishment candidates. Throughout the summer and fall of 2015, the top tier included three antiestablishment candidates who have never held political office: real estate mogul and reality television star Donald Trump, retired pediatric neurosurgeon Dr. Ben Carson, and former Hewlett-Packard CEO Carly Fiorina.

Donald Trump (Joseph Sohm/Shutterstock)

Dr. Ben Carson (Albert H. Teich/Shutterstock)

Trump catapulted to the top of polls following the inauguration of his campaign in June, and, despite what most political pundits considered numerous public gaffes, maintained frontrunner status in most, but not all, polls through the fall of 2015. Trump continued to defy so-called political experts, who continually predicted the demise of his campaign, by employing seemingly inflammatory rhetoric, including his assertions that Mexican immigrants are criminals and drug dealers, his swipe at Senator John McCain's (R-AZ) military service and years as a POW in Vietnam, and what many considered sexist attacks against Fox News anchor Megyn Kelly. Trump's no-holds-barred campaign style, along with his campaign theme of "Make America Great Again!" and refusal to adhere to political correctness, resonated with Republican and independent voters who had tired of the same old Washington insiders. Trump not only routinely topped national and early-state polls but also dominated political news coverage, particularly on cable news. Among the top issues on which Trump focused were illegal immigration and job creation.

Similarly, both Carson and Fiorina gained media attention and traction in polls for not sounding like typical politicians, thereby campaigning as legitimate outsiders. Carson's message on the campaign trail appealed particularly to social conservatives, as he touted his stance as a pro-life candidate who wanted to balance the federal budget, grant local control on education policies, and repeal the Affordable Care Act. Carson also focused on the need for America to embrace its Judeo-Christian roots, a message that made him a favorite with the so-called Christian Right. Many experts predicted that Carson would do well in Iowa since a majority of Republican caucus participants identify themselves as social conservative and/or evangelical Christians. Carson's campaign message had similarities to those of two previous Republican winners of the Iowa Caucuses—former Arkansas Governor Mike Huckabee in 2008 and former Pennsylvania Senator Rick Santorum in 2012. Ironically, while both Huckabee and Santorum were running again for the 2016 Republican nomination, neither was able to break through as a top-tier candidate, despite their previous victories in Iowa.

As the only woman in a crowded Republican field, Fiorina focused on her corporate experience and the need to put a non-career politician in the White House. She gained momentum in the polls following her impressive performance in the first two Republican debates. While she was relegated to the "undercard" debate in August, media pundits were unanimous in their assessment that she won that contest. Her narrative attracted more media attention in the ensuing weeks, which increased her standing in numerous polls, thus enabling her to secure a spot on the main debate stage in the second GOP debate in September on CNN. Following that debate, pundits again said she had clearly won the night, and her performance drove up her numbers in various polls, ranking her anywhere from second to fourth within the entire Republican field. Yet, her momentum began to stall as her poll numbers plateaued in late

October despite another strong performance in the third GOP debate that month. She was often labeled a strong candidate but was never viewed as a favorite to win a particular state on the primary map. Instead, many believed she was instead positioning herself as a potential running mate or cabinet appointee in a future Republican administration.

Carly Fiorina (AP Photo/John Minchillo)

Beyond the antiestablishment wing of the Republican field, several experienced politicians stayed in the mix of top-tier candidates through the fall of 2015. Those included former Florida Governor Jeb Bush (son of President George H. W. Bush and brother of President George W. Bush), Florida Senator Marco Rubio, Ohio Governor John Kasich, Texas Senator Ted Cruz, and New Jersey Governor Chris Christie. Many political experts expected Bush to be the frontrunner, especially given the vast resources amassed by the pro-Bush Super PAC Right to Rise USA, which raised $103 million during the first six months of 2015 (which greatly outpaced Super PAC fundraising of any other candidate).[3] However, throughout the summer and fall, Bush struggled to gain ground in public opinion polls, not least because many believed that his last name, especially as associated with his brother's presidency, continued to slow his campaign. Bush also did not generate as much excitement on the campaign trail as some of his antiestablishment rivals, which wasn't helped by his relatively moderate positions on issues such as immigration reform and the educational reform initiative Common Core. Bush famously quipped in early 2015 that the Republican nominee would need to "lose the primary to win the general election," referring to the increasing need to appeal to the base of the party in the primaries and to the center in the general election.[4] By the end of October, despite Bush's early fundraising advantage and name recognition, his campaign was forced to cut payroll and staff positions as part of a downsizing effort.[5]

Jeb Bush (Andrew Cline/Shutterstock)

Marco Rubio (Rich Koele/Shutterstock)

Among the other Republican candidates, Rubio offered a more youthful, energetic message and also emphasized his personal story. As the son of Cuban immigrants and from a working-class background, Rubio was the second-youngest candidate to seek the presidency during the 2016 campaign (both he and Louisiana Governor Bobby Jindal were born in 1971; Rubio in May and Jindal in June), one of only four generation X candidates (Walker and Cruz rounded out the generational group), and one of only two Hispanic candidates on either side (the other being Cruz). In addition, Rubio had strong debate performances throughout the fall, and pundits agreed that he was the winner of the third GOP debate in late October. As the popular second-term governor of the important swing state of Ohio, Kasich, one of the last Republican contenders to enter the race in June 2015, struggled to gain traction in the early fall months. Yet, he touted his experience as both a former member of Congress (he chaired the Budget Committee during the late 1990s, when the bipartisan efforts of the Republican-led House and President Bill Clinton balanced the federal budget), and his accomplishments during his six years as Ohio governor, for example, debt reduction and job creation. Many pundits also recognized the importance of Ohio as a swing state, so they viewed his presence on a Republican ticket, either as a presidential or vice presidential nominee, as a clear electoral advantage, especially since no Republican had ever won the presidency without winning the state of Ohio in the general election (and no Democrat had won the presidency without Ohio since John F. Kennedy in 1960). Kasich was also the first candidate to announce a federal debt-reduction plan, one, he claimed, that would eliminate the federal debt within eight years.

John Kasich (Office of Ohio Governor John R. Kasich)

Cruz and Christie remained longshots to capture the nomination throughout the fall, yet both proved to be skilled campaigners and excellent public speakers with quite different appeal to voters. Cruz labeled himself as an antiestablishment candidate who appeals to the Christian conservative base of the party and who has not been afraid to take on the Republican leadership in Washington. Political experts agreed that Trump's presence in the race cut into possible support for Cruz among those voters disaffected by the Republican Party establishment in Washington. Christie was seen as a more moderate Republican who could leverage his ability to get things done as a Republican governor of a solid Democratic state, and his past experience as a U.S. attorney soon after the 9/11 terrorist attacks.

Ted Cruz (Albert H. Teich/Shutterstock)

Among the candidates who failed to resonate with a wide spectrum of voters was Kentucky Senator Rand Paul, who, despite his early entrance in the race in April and his libertarian viewpoints on numerous issues, failed to capture the excitement that his father, Congressman Ron Paul, had when he ran for president in 2008 and 2012. (The elder Paul appealed not only to fiscal conservatives with his ideas about smaller government but also to independents and young voters who disapproved of U.S. foreign policy intervention around the globe). Rounding out the field of Republican contenders, and those who failed to break through to the top tier in terms of money raised, media coverage, or polling, included Huckabee, Santorum, Jindal (who dropped out of the race in mid-November), South Carolina Senator Lindsey Graham, former New York Governor George Pataki, and former Virginia Governor Jim Gilmore.

The Candidates: Democrats

On the Democratic side, what once seemed an inevitable victory for Hillary Clinton in the race for her party's nomination took on a different narrative once the story broke in March 2015 about the private e-mail server that she kept in her Chappaqua, New York, home while serving as secretary of state (2009–2013). Stories about whether she stored classified material on the nongovernment server, whether that classified information was passed through unsecure channels, whether anyone without proper security clearance had access to that information, whether hackers had breached the system, and whether she deleted work-related e-mails after saying in a press conference back in March 2015 that she did not continued to dog her campaign. Questions also continued to be raised about possible conflicts of interest between her duties as secretary of state and associations with controversial financial contributors to the Clinton Foundation. The ongoing FBI investigation of the private server and the possible deletions of relevant e-mails and their attempted retrieval by government officials kept the possibility of federal investigations and grand jury indictments alive and well in media coverage. Clinton's responses about the issue were not always consistent and were at times sarcastic or flip (when asked by Fox News' Ed Henry if her server had been wiped clean, she responded, "You mean with a cloth or something?"). As a result, throughout the summer and early fall, Clinton's

support plummeted in numerous polls, as a majority of voters not only found her dishonest and

untrustworthy but also increasingly viewed her as a negative rather than positive candidate. Yet,

Clinton has remained the presumptive frontrunner for the Democrats: She has locked up a

majority of big Democratic donors, she has the best campaign infrastructure, and the Democratic

Party has a rather shallow bench in terms of presidential candidates this time around.

Hillary Clinton (United States Department of State)

While Clinton's campaign has been hampered by what many have referred to as

an enthusiasm gap, and voters have succumbed to what, over the years, has become known as

"Clinton fatigue" (resulting from the numerous personal and political scandals surrounding the

Clintons since they first appeared on the national stage in 1991), the excitement over Senator

Bernie Sanders (VT) has been palpable and genuine, as evidenced by the tens of thousands of attendees at his campaign rallies. During the summer, Sanders attracted large numbers at numerous venues around the country, while Clinton's attendance figures flagged, such as the mere 5,000 that witnessed her "reboot," that is, the campaign kick-off in New York (which had followed a video launch of her campaign in April), where the overflow room sat empty. Sanders, a self-described democratic socialist, turned out to be more competitive on the Democratic side than most predicted. His campaign message about income inequality, Wall Street reform, a minimum wage hike, and free college tuition, among other progressive issues, resonated with the liberal base of the Democratic Party and many young voters as well. Despite serving in Congress (both the House and the Senate) since 1991, Sanders has benefited from the antiestablishment fervor among voters on the left in a similar way that Trump, Carson, and Fiorina have with voters on the right. There has been an energy and excitement attached to the Sanders campaign that Clinton's has lacked; polls routinely show that voters perceive Sanders to be more honest, authentic, and consistent in his positions than Clinton. He has also shown himself to be a skilled fundraiser as well. At the end of the third quarter of 2015, while the Clinton campaign bragged about its $29 million haul, the Sanders campaign countered by raising $26 million during the same three-month period. Given Sanders' reliance on smaller donations (reminiscent of Barack Obama's early fundraising success in 2007), the third-quarter sum highlighted his viability and competitiveness as a serious candidate on the eve of the official primary season.[6]

Bernie Sanders (Juli Hansen/Shutterstock)

Speculation persisted about a possible late entry into the race by Vice President Joe Biden throughout most of October, but on October 21 Biden finally announced that he would not run. Incumbent vice presidents are often considered strong contenders for their party's nomination, and Biden had already run for president twice before (in 1988 and 2008). However, the death of Biden's oldest son, Beau Biden, in May 2015 of brain cancer at the age of 46, became a principal reason for Biden's decision not to run. In addition, a late entry would have been problematic in terms of campaign infrastructure and fundraising. Media speculation also hit a fevered pitch at times over which candidate—Biden or Clinton—would gain Obama's endorsement, as both had been key figures in his administration. Many reporters and pundits got the story wrong in the end. *New York Times* columnist Maureen Dowd wrote in August about how Beau had urged his father to run for the presidency prior to his death, and subsequent news coverage conflated that to a death-bed plea to run. After announcing that he would not run, Biden stated in an interview with *60 Minutes* that the media claims were not true, and that while his son thought he could win, there had been no "Hollywood-esque" moment as others had reported.[7]

Joe Biden (David Lienemann/White House)

The remaining Democratic candidates received minimal attention, as media coverage focused on the presumptive nominee, Clinton, and her nagging political problems, Sanders's surprising competitiveness, and Biden's possible entry into the race. Those candidates included former Maryland Governor Martin O'Malley, former Virginia Senator Jim Webb, former Rhode Island Governor and Senator Lincoln Chaffee, and academic and attorney Lawrence Lessig. After the first Democratic debate in mid-October (for which Lessig did not qualify due to low poll numbers), both Webb and Chaffee ended their campaigns. Lessig would soon follow by dropping out on November 2. While pundits declared Clinton the winner of the first debate, other polling and focus groups declared Sanders the winner. By early November, the race for the Democratic nomination seemed destined to be a two-person race between Clinton as the presumed frontrunner and establishment candidate and Sanders as a grassroots progressive alternative. Much of the storyline about Clinton had been shaped by both good and bad news. The good reflected her putatively strong debate performance and her assured demeanor during her 11-hour testimony before the House Select Benghazi Committee, which resulted in no further damage, at least in the short term, to her campaign and her standing among her core Democratic supporters. Both factors, along with Biden's decision not to run, culminated in what many media pundits called her best week of the campaign. The bad, however, came from the ongoing FBI investigation into her use of a private e-mail server and the competitiveness of the Sanders campaign, a development that few political experts could have predicted at the start of 2015.

Fundraising

While making accurate predictions during the pre-nomination period is a risky proposition, there are several factors that can help determine the viability of candidates. One of the most important things to consider is fundraising and whether candidates can attract both large and small donors. In addition, campaign organization and a competent ground game (which includes volunteers who focus on, among other things, voter registration and turnout) demonstrate candidate viability and campaign strength. These can provide early momentum heading into the first state contests. Throughout the summer months and into the fall of 2015, both Clinton and Bush outpaced their competitors in overall fundraising. Clinton had the highest money totals from contributions directly to her campaign (more than $77 million through September 2015), while Bush had an enormous lead in Super PAC donations (more than $108 million through July 2015). However, winning the money primary left neither as a lock for their party's respective nominations. What fundraising numbers can do, however, is not only determine which first-tier candidates are viable but also show which second-tier candidates lack viability, which usually encourages some of these second-tier candidates to withdraw from the race. Tables 1 and 2 show fundraising totals, from most to least, as reported by the Federal Election Commission (FEC) in October 2015. Tables 3 and 4 show Super PAC totals through July 31, 2015, as reported by the FEC. Based on the FEC figures provided in mid-October 2015, candidates in both the Democratic and Republican fields (including the two candidates who had already dropped out) raised an aggregate of nearly $300 million, while candidate-specific Super PACs had already raised an aggregate of more than $255 million.

One of the most interesting points to note from the 2015 money primary is the fact that Walker's campaign had raised more than $7 million and had received Super PAC support for more than $20 million by the time he had dropped out of the presidential contest in September. The short tenure of Walker's campaign shows that nearly $30 million in campaign funds does not guarantee a candidate's success. Similarly, Perry had close to $14 million in Super PAC funding prior to his exit from the Republican race. Some candidates, such as Carson and Cruz, benefited from a strong antiestablishment mood among both large and small Republican donors. And Trump, the frontrunner in polls throughout the fall of 2015, relied heavily on his own money to fund his campaign, placing his fundraising numbers in the middle of the Republican pack.

On the Democratic side, Clinton raised more money than any candidate during the pre-nomination period, but, according to FEC data, she also led all candidates in campaign spending. Between July 1 and September 30, her campaign spent $26 million—more than twice the amount spent by any other presidential candidate—on campaign infrastructure, which includes payroll, office space, and polling. A significant concern for the Clinton campaign with respect to Clinton's "increasingly tapped-out big donor base" is whether she can find additional big donors to keep her campaign afloat through the end of the primary season. Only 17 percent of Clinton donors gave $200 or less; this problem is similar to what she experienced in 2008, when after maxing out among large donors she was forced to loan several million dollars of her own money to her campaign.[8] She also ended her failed bid for the nomination in 2008 with a total of $20 million in campaign debt, which was not completely paid off until January 2013.[9] Again, while money in the pre-nomination phase is one key element to consider, having large sums of money to spend does not guarantee electoral success.

Table 1: 2015 Fundraising Totals—Republicans

Total Money Raised by Republican Candidates, through September 30, 2015

Candidate	Third-Quarter Totals (7/1/15–9/30/15)	Total Amount Raised
Ben Carson	$20,767,266	$31,409,508
Ted Cruz	$12,218,137	$26,567,298
Marco Rubio	$5,724,784	$25,328,081
Jeb Bush	$13,384,832	$24,814,729
Rand Paul	$2,509,251	$9,442,030
Carly Fiorina	$6,791,308	$8,496,012
Scott Walker	$7,379,170	$7,379,170
Donald Trump	$3,926,511	$5,828,922
Lindsey Graham	$1,052,657	$4,762,210
John Kasich	$4,376,787	$4,376,787
Chris Christie	$4,208,984	$4,208,984

Mike Huckabee	$1,241,737	$3,246,200
Rick Perry	$287,199	$1,426,683
Bobby Jindal	$579,438	$1,158,196
Rick Santorum	$387,985	$1,012,659
George Pataki	$153,513	$409,308
Jim Gilmore	$105,807	$105,807

Source: Federal Election Commission

Table 2: 2015 Fundraising Totals—Democrats

Total Money Raised by Democratic Candidates, through September 30, 2015

Candidate	Third-Quarter Totals (7/1/15–9/30/15)	Total Amount Raised
Hillary Clinton	$29,921,653	$77,471,603
Bernie Sanders	$26,216,430	$41,463,783
Martin O'Malley	$1,282,820	$3,289,725
Lawrence Lessig	$1,016,189	$1,016,189
Jim Webb	$696,972	$696,972
Lincoln Chaffee	$15,457	$15,457

Source: Federal Election Commission

Table 3: 2015 Super PAC Donations—Republicans

Total Money Raised for Republican Candidates, through July 31, 2015

Candidate	Total
Jeb Bush	$108,500,000
Ted Cruz	$38,400,000
Scott Walker	$20,000,000
Marco Rubio	$17,300,000
Chris Christie	$14,400,000
Rick Perry	$13,800,000
Rand Paul	$6,900,000
Mike Huckabee	$4,500,000
Bobby Jindal	$3,700,000
Carly Fiorina	$3,500,000
Lindsey Graham	$2,900,000
George Pataki	$900,000
Rick Santorum	$300,000
Ben Carson	$200,000
John Kasich	$0
Donald Trump	$0
Jim Gilmore	$0

Source: Federal Election Commission/*New York Times*

Table 4: 2015 Super PAC Donations—Democrats

Total Money Raised for Democratic Candidates, through July 31, 2015

Candidate	Total
Hillary Clinton	$20,300,000
Martin O'Malley	$300,000
Bernie Sanders	$0
Lawrence Lessig	$0
Jim Webb	$0
Lincoln Chaffee	$0

Source: Federal Election Commission/*New York Times*

Polls

While money alone cannot determine success during the pre-nomination phase, polls cannot guarantee the probability of nomination either. Countless opinion polls, conducted by this or that polling organization, promote their predictive value, but they cannot accurately predict prospective voter behavior based on results obtained during the pre-nomination period. National polls during this phase are meaningless, as party nomination is a product of the accumulated results from individual state contests. Nonetheless, this reality does nothing to abate the proliferation of early national polls and the attention devoted to them by leading media outlets. For better or worse, the relentless focus on the latest polls and their results has become a permanent staple of the pre-nomination phase of presidential primaries. Furthermore, not all polls are created equal; reliability, accuracy, and representativeness invariably depend on the viability of several methodological parameters, not the least of which are sample size and voter type. For example, a sample of more than 1,000 "likely" (as opposed to "registered") voters will be more accurate and representative than one of just 400 respondents, which may or may not distinguish between likely and registered voters. (This is only one example of how methodology and research design can affect the accuracy and the predictive power of polls.) Unfortunately, media coverage of polls is largely indiscriminate, with little or no distinction made among the different types of polling methodologies.

A high standing in a September or October 2015 poll cannot guarantee support from voters come February 2016. This is particularly true for Trump, who may have dominated Republican polls and media coverage (because of name recognition and his unrestrained criticism of the Washington establishment that makes for good headlines) in the fall of 2015, but it was unclear whether his poll numbers reflected registered or likely voters in primary contests. Also, as Clinton's numbers regarding likeability and voting preference demonstrate, the relationship between the two is hardly intuitive or predictable at this stage of the game. Despite Clinton's flagging poll numbers on questions of trust and honesty, based on poll results, she was still considered the Democratic frontrunner throughout the fall of 2015. Various political websites provide aggregate polling results, such as RealClearPolitics (which started the trend in 2002), which pools results from various sources to provide greater reliability and, it is hoped, accuracy regarding voter preferences for upcoming contests. Still, in mid-November, with less than 100 days until the Iowa Caucuses, aggregate polling provided a snapshot of the pre-nomination phase yet offered few definitive predictions (See Tables 5 and 6).

Table 5: Aggregate National Poll Results—Republican Candidates

Candidate	Percentage
Donald Trump	27.5
Ben Carson	19.8
Marco Rubio	12.5
Ted Cruz	11.3
Jeb Bush	5.5
Carly Fiorina	3.5
Mike Huckabee	3.3
Chris Christie	3.0
John Kasich	2.8
Rand Paul	2.5
Lindsey Graham	0.8
George Pataki	0.8
Rick Santorum	0.5
Jim Gilmore	0.0

Source: RealClearPolitics, November 22, 2015.[12]

Table 6: Aggregate National Poll Results—Democratic Candidates

Candidate	Percentage
Hillary Clinton	55.8
Bernie Sanders	30.2
Martin O'Malley	4.4

Source: RealClearPolitics, November 22, 2015.[13]

Debates

As with a candidate's position in pre-nomination polls, debate performance can be a poor judge of electoral success or medium-term to long-term viability, nor can it by itself assure a victory in specific primary contests. Whether during the pre-nomination phase, primary election voting in the spring of the presidential election year, or general election, debates are more often about political theater and media sound bites than substantive policy discussions. While media outlets routinely declare respective debate winners, such conclusions do not arise from objective data analysis but from the subjective evaluations of media pundits. The misconception that debate performance and electoral success are related is fortified by the fact that debates are now a permanent part of the pre-nomination phase of the campaign, so voters and pundits cannot help but regard them as valid predictors of electoral effectiveness. With each successive debate the misconception is reinforced, which undermines reliance on more objective means of candidate assessment.

Republicans had six debates prior to the first contest, which takes place in Iowa in February of the election year. Needless to say, the large Republican field posed quite a challenge for debate organizers, party officials, and the candidates themselves, as each candidate tried to optimize his or her opportunity while, at the same time, debate organizers attempted to manage and divide such a large field of candidates effectively. The first Republican debate in August 2015, hosted by Fox News, was based on qualification criteria also employed at the subsequent debate venues, using poll numbers and corresponding candidate positions to divide the field into two more manageable groups. An earlier (not in prime time) debate was devoted to those candidates with the lowest poll numbers, while a later (prime time) one was reserved for the top contenders. The second GOP debate in September, hosted by CNN, had the largest field—11 candidates—on the prime-time debate stage, which was held at the Ronald Reagan Presidential Library in Simi Valley, California, with Air Force One as the backdrop. The third GOP debate, hosted by CNBC, in Colorado at the end of October was notable for the contentious atmosphere between candidates and moderators, as the heavily criticized moderators asked "gotcha" questions focused more on personal attacks than on substantive policies. The fourth GOP debate, hosted by Fox Business News in November, saw a return to more substantive policy discussions.

Republican Presidential Candidates (Joseph Sohm/Shutterstock)

On the Democratic side, fewer debates were scheduled and the first one did not occur until October. Many Democrats disapproved of the debate schedule submitted by Democratic National Committee Chair Debbie Wasserman Schultz (also a member of the House of Representatives from Florida), because the party wound up with fewer debates than the GOP, which, to compound the problem, began at a later date than those of the rival party. Notably, both the Sanders and O'Malley campaigns complained that their requests for additional debates had been ignored. Some, particularly within the O'Malley campaign, believed that Wasserman Schultz, who had co-chaired Clinton's presidential campaign in 2008, scheduled fewer debates (only four before the Iowa Caucuses) and only one with a weeknight prime-time spot (the first debate in October) to give an advantage to Clinton as the presumed frontrunner. (The theory being that the fewer the debates with fewer voters watching, the fewer opportunities other candidates would have to attack Clinton and her frontrunner status.) The remaining Democratic debates were scheduled for either a Saturday or Sunday, which placed them in direct competition for viewers with NFL and college football broadcasts. Indeed, the second Democratic debate, held on November 14 in Des Moines, Iowa, and hosted by CBS News, had the lowest viewership of any debate to date during this campaign season.

Democratic Debate (Joseph Sohm/Shutterstock)

Conclusion

The bottom line is that while political junkies love all the early coverage and gamesmanship of the pre-nomination period, the road to the general election and the selection of the next president is a long one whose conclusion usually differs from the jockeying for power, influence, and voters that mark the earliest parts of presidential campaigns. If the history of presidential campaigns has taught us nothing else, it is that anything can happen between the pre-nomination phase of a campaign and the actual election in November 2016.

Notes

1. See Arthur Hadley, *The Invisible Primary* (Englewood Cliffs, NJ: Prentice-Hall, 1976).

2. Philip Bump, "Scott Walker's Presidential Bid Was the Shortest in at Least Two Decades," *Washington Post*, September 22, 2015, http://www.washingtonpost.com/news/the-fix/wp/2015/09/22/scott-walkers-presidential-bid-was-the-shortest-in-two-decades/.

3. Tarini Parti, "Jeb Super PAC Raises $103 Million," *Politico*, July 31, 2015,

    http://www.politico.com/story/2015/07/jeb-bush-superpac-103-million-2016-120853.

4. Michael J. Mishak, "Jeb Bush's 'Lose the Primary to Win the General' Could Just Mean 'Lose

    the Primary,'" *National Journal*, June 15, 2015,

    http://www.nationaljournal.com/twentysixteen/2015/06/15/Jeb-Bushs-Lose-Primary-

    Win-General-Could-Just-Mean-Lose-Primary.

5. David Jackson, "Jeb Bush's Struggling Campaign Cuts Pay, Staff Positions," *USA Today*,

    October 23, 2015, http://onpolitics.usatoday.com/2015/10/23/jeb-bush-cuts-pay-staff-

    positions/?dlvrit=384245.

6. Jessica Mendoza, "Bernie Sanders' $26 Million Haul Proves He's a Serious Challenger,"

    Christian Science Monitor, October 1, 2015,

    http://www.csmonitor.com/USA/Politics/2015/1001/Bernie-Sanders-26-million-haul-

    proves-he-s-a-serious-challenger-video.

7. Eric Bradner, "Biden: My Talk with Beau about Running Was No 'Hollywood Moment,'"

    CNN, October 26, 2015, http://www.cnn.com/2015/10/25/politics/joe-biden-decision-not-

    to-run-family/index.html.

8. Kenneth P. Vogel, Isaac Arnsdorf, and Theodoric Mayer, "Hillary's Cash Flow Issue,"

    Politico, October 16, 2015, http://www.politico.com/story/2015/10/hillary-clinton-fec-

    filing-cash-flow-problem-214870.

9. Catalina Carnia, "Hillary Clinton Pays Off 2008 Campaign Debt," *USA Today*, January 23,

    2013, http://www.usatoday.com/story/onpolitics/2013/01/23/hillary-clinton-campaign-

    debt-free/1857991/.

10. "Which Presidential Candidates Are Winning the Money Race," *New York Times*, updated

    October 16, 2015, http://www.nytimes.com/interactive/2016/us/elections/election-2016-

    campaign-money-race.html?ref=politics&_r=0.

11. Ibid.

12. "Polls: 2016 Republican Nomination," available at

    http://www.realclearpolitics.com/epolls/2016/president/us/2016_republican_presidential_

    nomination-3823.html.

13. Polls: 2016 Democratic Nomination," available at

    http://www.realclearpolitics.com/epolls/2016/president/us/2016_democratic_presidential

    _nomination-3824.html.

Chapter 3

WINNING THE NOMINATION

The pre-nomination phase demonstrates the candidates' "behind the scenes" strength, revealed through their fundraising, endorsements, and name recognition. Clinton easily won this phase for the Democrats, despite the excitement generated by Sanders. On the Republican side, Trump clearly walked away with the lion's share of attention from the media and the public. In terms of endorsements and fundraising, Carson, Cruz, Rubio, and Bush dominated. However, as candidates inevitably learn, success during the early stages of the campaign does not necessarily translate into success at the ballot box during primary contests. Primaries and caucuses are confined by institutional rules, the logic of the electoral calendar, and state-specific get-out-the-vote strategies for which many pre-nomination poll leaders lack both the political wherewithal and the organizational skill necessary for success. With the changes made to both the rules and calendar, as well as changes in demographics, each presidential nominating cycle yields its own drama and unexpected outcomes—2016 is no exception. As they say in sports, it's why we play the game.

The Calendar

In every state in the union, plus Washington, DC, Puerto Rico, Guam, American Samoa, and the US Virgin Islands, the political parties schedule their primaries or caucuses. In some states, the Republican and Democratic Parties have their contests on the same day; in other states, they are on different days. The scheduled date of a primary or caucus does not seem like a big deal, but the date can have a dramatic influence on the outcome of the race, or it could have no impact on a race that has already been decided. Thus, the scheduling of primaries and caucuses has become a huge strategic opportunity for both states and candidates.

In 2008, in response to the fact that neither an incumbent president nor vice president was in the race, state parties were especially intent on influencing the race, making the biggest impact, and shaping electoral momentum, so every state wanted its primary to be scheduled as early as possible. Florida, like many other states, moved up their primaries to ensure their choice influenced the outcome. In years past, the race for the nomination could end early with big wins or big momentum shifts. As shown in Table 7, in 2000 and 2004, Iowa and New Hampshire had their caucus and primary traditionally in late January or early February. However, in 2008 and 2012 that changed dramatically. The earlier schedule in 2008 and 2012 heightened the drama for the voters and the media, but the compacted schedule made campaigning difficult for the candidates, as it compressed the opportunity to build momentum (known as the bandwagon effect), and forced candidates to spend a lot of money early in the race.

The 2016 calendar is a reversal of the dramatic changes from 2008 and a return to a pre-2000 approach as it ends extreme frontloading with the contest running from February 1 to June 30. Both parties wanted to avoid intense campaigning during the December holidays, when presidential politics is the furthest thing from voters' minds.

Table 7: Changes to the Calendar/Number of Contests per Month

	2000	2004	2008	2012	2016
Iowa	Jan. 24	Jan. 19	Jan. 3	Jan. 3	Feb. 1
New Hampshire	Feb. 2	Jan. 27	Jan. 8	Jan. 10	Feb. 9
January	1	5	8	4	0
February	12	24	40	6	4
March	34	23	7	22	32
April	4	3	2	8	8
May	10	7	8	8	6
June	5	7	4	6	7
Total*	66	69	69	54	58**

Source: *New York Times*
* Each year has a different number of primaries and caucuses because some get cancelled, and some states combine their primaries while other states split them.
** As of November 2, 2015, four Republican caucuses had not been scheduled.

Both national parties agreed in 2014 to push back the start of the nominating calendar and to also encourage the state party organizations not to frontload the calendar. The parties were successful in pushing back the start of the calendar but did not have much success dispersing the contests. In 2008, February was the big month where roughly half of all nominating contests were held (Super Tuesday was labeled as Tsunami Tuesday that year). In 2016, March will be the make or break month for many candidates. So many southern states have signed up for March 1 that the date is being nicknamed the SEC primary since, like the college athletic Southeastern Conference, that date will also include Arkansas, Georgia, Alabama, Kentucky,

Louisiana, Tennessee, and Texas. (The southern states of Virginia and Oklahoma are also voting that day but are not part of the SEC in the world of college athletics). So much attention has been paid to the SEC primary that the event even has a twitter feed and a website.[1] With the Florida primary scheduled for March 15, the South will have a much louder voice in the outcome of the presidential nomination than in previous years. This could benefit candidates with southern roots, such as Bush and Rubio of Florida and Cruz of Texas. Although, it is important to remember that a regional bloc strategy can also backfire as it did in 1988, when several candidates in both parties split the vote.

On the Democratic side, Clinton could amass enough pledged delegates by mid-March to make the rest of the contests irrelevant. However, on the Republican side, if two or more candidates split Iowa, New Hampshire, and South Carolina (also in February), it is unlikely any candidate will have achieved enough momentum to build a bandwagon effect and sweep the March contests. If two or three candidates earn victories in March, yielding a split in momentum, the Republican search for a nominee could continue well into June. In that scenario, where every state outcome could be significant and determinant of the outcome, citizens and democracy benefit. However, for the candidates and the party, it means a long drawn-out battle that highlights divisions within, provides fodder for the general election opponent, and burns through an enormous amount of money.

The timing of the nominating debates also reveals a bit about the Republican Party elite's thinking about the process. To winnow the field, the Republicans scheduled six debates between August and December of 2015—typically that is before most Americans are focused on the campaign—but is when the insiders and party voters begin making choices about whom to support if they haven't already. Into 2016, the Republicans scheduled six debates that match the caucus and primary calendar. There are four debates firmly on the calendar in the states of Iowa, New Hampshire, South Carolina, and Texas. Two more debates are tentatively scheduled in March. The fact that they do not have firm dates or cities associated with those debates indicates that the party is hoping the February and March 1 primaries and caucuses will have shrunk the pool of candidates enough so that additional debates will not be necessary.

Although the parties pushed back and encouraged spreading out the primary and caucus calendar, both parties decided to hold their conventions in July, which is earlier than normal. Usually, the conventions are later in August, closer to the start of the general election. There were two reasons for the change in dates. First, the 2016 Rio de Janeiro Summer Olympics will be held August 5–21. No party or candidate wants to compete with the media saturation that goes along with the Olympic Games. However, if a candidate could successfully drape himself or herself in the heightened patriotism that occurs during an Olympics, the candidate could benefit enormously from the switch from negativity to positivity. The second reason for the early conventions originates with Mitt Romney's tough win of the Republican nomination in 2012. Romney spent a considerable amount of money to gain the nomination and was left with only $5 million on hand before he could tap the enormous amount of general election money raised. The long, tough fight also forced him to shift his political stances to the right, more in line with the core Republican Party primary voters. Party insiders believed the combination of being short of money and being forced to articulate more conservative stances weakened him with undecided voters in the general election.[2]

The Rules

The nomination is awarded at the party's national convention to the candidate who has surpassed the delegate threshold established by each party. Thus, the state parties' and national parties' rules for awarding and counting delegates matter significantly for both the states and the candidates. In order to retain control of the calendar, the parties rewarded states with bonus delegates at the convention if they ran their primary later in the calendar. In addition, the national parties' rules now prevent states from using winner-take-all primaries until after March 15. So, states had to decide if they wanted to award all their convention delegates to one candidate, or did they want to provide a proportional allocation of their delegates, or did they want to do a hybrid of the two? Proportional allocation, depending on the rules of each state, typically matches the popular vote. Winner-take-all contests typically encourage a quicker outcome as a candidate can build an insurmountable lead while proportional allocation allows for greater shifting of momentum.

The Republican Party has a total of 2,472 delegates at stake; a candidate needs 1,237 to win the nomination. The Democratic Party has a total of 4,491 delegates at stake, so a candidate needs 2,246 to win. However, not all delegates are the same. According to the rules of the convention, Republicans have at-large delegates (AL) which are "statewide delegates who are residents of that state and are selected at large. Each state receives 10 AL delegates plus additional AL delegates based on the state's past Republican electoral successes. . . . Congressional District (CD) Delegates must be residents of and selected by the congressional district they represent. Each state gets three CD delegates per district . . . RNC Members are automatically national convention delegates and include the state's national committeeman, national committeewoman, and state chair."[3]

The Democratic national rules for delegate allocation are even more complicated. They have four separate categories of delegates: district-level delegates, at-large delegates, pledged PLEOs (party leaders and elected officials), and unpledged PLEOs (so-called super delegates).[4] For 2016, there are a total of 713 super delegates. Hillary Clinton learned in 2008 how important the super delegates were as she eventually won more votes in the primaries (18 million to Barack Obama's 17.6 million), but she trailed in momentum, and ultimately, she lost to Obama by less than 100 delegates.

Although the national party makes the rules for its total delegate count and its convention, it is the state parties that make the rules for everything from what to have (primary, convention, caucus), when to have it, and how to allocate their delegates. The first choice each state party makes centers on what kind of contest they want to have to award their state's share of delegates. States can have primaries, caucuses, conventions, or a hybrid of the options. Most states have primaries, which are secret ballot elections. Caucuses are gatherings where preferences for a candidate are expressed and then counted. The choice of what kind of contest to hold and when to hold it is influenced by strategic choices and by national and state party rules.

The second choice a state must make is about participation. Is your state party contest open to all citizens regardless of party affiliation, is it closed to only members of the party, or is it a mix of open and closed? In 2016, 42 percent of primaries and caucuses are closed, 29 percent are open, and 29 percent are mixed or hybrids of the two. Closed primaries and caucuses are the norm because the process is about selecting a choice for the party's leader. The party has to be cautious about allowing independents and individuals who do not affiliate with the party to have input choosing their leadership. It can be attractive to independents or people who affiliate with the party but don't often participate to see someone at odds with the party elites. For example, in

39

2015, Trump took positions not traditionally associated with the Republican orthodoxy, and he said numerous things that fall outside "political correctness"; the combination should have spelled disaster for his candidacy, yet millions tuned in to see him in the Republican debates and he led in the polls for months. It remains to be seen if traditional Republicans who make up the primary and caucus electorate are will actually vote for the nontraditional candidacy of Trump.

The third choice a state must make is determining the winner of the contest—winner take all or proportional allocation. Not surprisingly, a state's decision whether to be winner take all or proportional includes in their calculus whether one of their own was a candidate or had hoped to be a candidate running for president. In Texas, with their junior senator (Cruz) running for president, the state decided to move up its primary to March 1, which meant the contest cannot be winner take all without incurring a penalty from the national party, but their proportional allocation is 80-20, which is nearly winner take all and will presumably benefit Cruz. In Florida, after getting heavily penalized in 2008 and 2012 for jumping ahead in the primary line, state officials made the strategic decision to be early in March but not so early that they could not move to a winner-take-all result. Thus, with a primary on March 15, the Florida primary is early enough to significantly affect momentum and potentially give a big boost to either Bush or Rubio. If both Bush and Rubio are still competitive at that point, they could also split the vote, opening the door for another candidate. Kentucky's rules change was perhaps the most overt decision to help "one of their own." Kentucky rules prevent a candidate from being on two different ballots at the same time. Paul is both up for reelection in the Senate and running for president. He and his supporters successfully petitioned the state Republican Party to switch to a caucus for the presidential nomination, which would allow him to run for both positions (though given Paul's standing in the prenominating phase, it seems unlikely this effort will be necessary).

Another seemingly minor but actually significant rule change is the Republican Party's decision to require that all caucus states allocate their delegates to the straw-vote winner. This is a direct response to 2012 where candidates, such as Rick Santorum and Newt Gingrich, won the vote but lost the delegate allocation in the state conventions that came later to candidates with strong on-the-ground organizations.[5] As a result, Iowa, Minnesota, Maine, and Washington made their caucus poll results binding. Two other states, Montana and Nebraska, went from nonbinding caucus/convention systems to winner-take-all primaries. The requirement that a state's delegates support the candidate that wins the caucus poll had the most interesting outcome in Colorado. Rather than have the presidential preference vote lock in delegates, Colorado decided to cancel the poll. It will still hold precinct caucus meetings to select their delegates, but the state's 37 delegates will not be pledged to a candidate. In the fiercely contested Democratic nomination contest between Clinton and Obama in 2008, having a pool of delegates unpledged could have significantly influenced the outcome. The Republican Party rule change tried to avoid the problems in 2012, but the end result has disenfranchised a group of Republicans because they do not want to commit early. Also, the lack of binding caucus results means Colorado will not see serious campaigning until the general election, despite having held one of the GOP debates in Boulder on October 28, 2015.

The Voters

In order to become president, a candidate must craft an appeal to very different kinds of voters. In the pre-nomination phase, candidates are trying to distinguish themselves amongst party elites and party insiders. During the nomination phase, candidates are still focused within their own party, trying to distinguish themselves from fellow party members. After winning the

41

nomination, the party's nominee then must turn to attracting independents, inattentive potential voters, and if really successful, voters aligned with the other party. The problem for the eventual nominee is that the appeals that distinguish themselves within the party often create divisions when focused on the general election.

Participation in primaries and caucuses relates strongly to the ease of participation in the process and the level of interest for potential voters. Ease of participation is all about what citizens have to do to participate. Primaries require citizens to show up and vote, while caucuses may require a slightly higher level of effort. For example, in Iowa, the Republican Caucus is simply a straw vote—a show of hands by those attending in each precinct. These results are used to elect delegates that go on to the 99 county conventions in support of the candidate receiving the most in the show of hands. The county conventions then elect delegates to go to the national convention in support of the party nominee. However, the Iowa Democratic Caucus rules require a lot more effort. Registered Democrats

gather at the precinct meeting places (there are close to 2,000 precincts statewide), supporters for each candidate have a chance to make their case, and then the participants gather into groups supporting particular candidates (undecided voters also cluster into a group). In order for a particular group to be viable, they must have a certain percentage of all the caucus participants. If they don't have enough people, the group disbands, and its members go to another group. The percentage cut-off is determined by the number of delegates assigned to the precinct. Democratic candidates must receive at least 15 percent of the votes in that precinct to move on to the county convention. If a candidate receives less than 15 percent of the votes, supporters of non-viable candidates have the option to join a viable candidate group, join another non-viable candidate group to become viable, join other groups to form an uncommitted group or chose to go nowhere and not be counted. Non-viable groups have up to 30 minutes to realign, if they fail to do so in that time, they can ask for more time, which is voted on by the caucus as a whole.[6]

Voting in the Iowa Caucus (Citizensharp/Wikimedia Commons)

As evident by what it takes to record your vote in the Iowa Democratic Caucus, voters in the nomination process are a special subset of voters in that they are both interested and active in the party. Unlike voters who only participate in the general election, primary and caucus voters pay attention to the process early. They typically are loyal to a party and want to choose their party's nominee. Early donors to a candidate will participate in the primary or caucus, as it makes no sense to donate and then not vote. The problem for most nomination voters is that the choice between candidates is typically narrow. Most of the candidates running for the nomination support the issues that are usually thought to define the Democrats and the Republicans. Republicans typically support less government regulation on economic issues and more regulation on social issues. Democrats typically support more regulation on business, particularly in favor of labor and the environment, and less social regulation. So the choice for the nominee is inside the choice already made—you have already decided to support this party, so the question now becomes, who to choose? After party affiliation, issue position and candidate characteristics tend to determine the outcome. Trust, style, and handling adversity are all personality traits that matter when the issue separation is so narrow.

Perhaps the biggest key to the nomination process is turnout. A large turnout, even in a close election, energizes the base of the party. The Democrats had enormous turnout in 2008 during the battle between Clinton and Obama, and that engagement carried through to the general election. The danger for the Democrats in 2016 is that with Clinton as the presumptive nominee before any vote is cast, Democratic voters do not get excited or activated in the process because they do not have to be. A sleepy, easy nomination battle is good for the candidate and is cheaper for the candidate, but it may not generate turnout in the general election.

We know from voting patterns, how people answer surveys, and from candidate strategy that voting behavior is linked to several demographic characteristics. While each voter is an individual, we do see patterns across demographics. These patterns yield a chicken and egg scenario—do voters from a demographic bloc vote that way because candidates appeal to them, or do candidates appeal to them because they vote a certain way? Table 8 shows how race and ethnicity might factor in the 2016 race. The data in Table 8 is based on the turnout, voting patterns, and exit polls from 2012. Using 2012, it is possible to predict demographic turnout in 2016. From 2012, it is clear that in total voter turnout, white voters still turn out in greater numbers than any other group. In addition, Republican voters are primarily white, while Democratic voters are more diverse with a mix of white, African American, Hispanic, and Asian voters. Hispanic voters remain the most attractive group for both parties. Unlike white and black America, Hispanic America is growing, and growing rapidly. However, they participate in politics at a much lower rate: less than 50 percent of eligible voters turn out.

Table 8 also demonstrates that the largest voting bloc, white voters, is not turning out in full. Imagine if 80 percent or 90 percent of African Americans and Hispanic voters turned out while only 50 percent of white and Asian American voters turned out. Would we get a different outcome at the polls? Would different issues take center stage on the campaign agenda? Absolutely, as campaigns and candidates serve those who participate. This is how voting holds public officials accountable. Turnout numbers help us understand which groups benefit from the public policies that elected officials enact.

The turnout numbers by income tell an even more significant story about accountability and winners and losers in the fight for public policies. According to the US Census Bureau, only 62 percent of voters with income levels of less than $50,000 dollars a year voted in 2012. In contrast, over 77 percent of voters with incomes higher than $75,000 dollars a year voted in 2012. As income goes up and down, the voting gap gets wider: "In the 2012 election, 80.2 percent of those making more than $150,000 voted, while only 46.9 percent of those making less than $10,000 voted."[7] Given the turnout disparities, it is not surprising that our policies and politics benefit wealthier individuals.

Table 8: Predicted Turnout in 2016

Demographic Group[8]	Turnout	Republican Votes	Democratic Votes
Non-Hispanic White	64.1%	55,456,129	36,663,687
African American	66.2%	1,064,812	16,391,123
Asian American and Other	49.3%	2,349,010	5,084,567
Hispanic	48.0%	4,183,299	10,973,582
Actual Popular Vote 2012[9]		60,933,504	65,915,795
Actual Popular Vote Percentage 2012		47.2%	51.06%

Source: RealClearPolitics and Federal Election Commission

Conventions

Once the primary and caucus votes have occurred there is one more thing to do: hold the national party convention. It used to be that serious politicking and brokering took place at the conventions, as deals with delegates were made to yield the nominee. In recent years, the conventions are more of an elaborate stage show to introduce the candidate. There is no suspense regarding the nominee because all the delegates' sorting and brokering have been kept to a minimum with the delegate math. The only suspense that remains at the convention is about the choice for the vice presidential candidate. The choice of a running mate is the first strategic decision the nominee makes. It will often say something about the holes a nominee is trying to fill in their resume. In 2008, Obama chose a seasoned politician and elder statesman in Biden, who had represented Delaware in the Senate since 1973, and who provided Obama a link to the traditional wing of the party that was intended to soothe voters worried about electing a younger man with little national experience. In contrast, McCain was at the time an elder statesman in the Republican Party, so he chose a younger woman from a western state, Governor Sarah Palin of Alaska.

John McCain and Sarah Palin at the 2008 Republican Convention (Alex Wong/EdStock)

In 2012, Romney also chose a younger running mate with Washington experience in Representative Paul Ryan of Wisconsin (a swing state). While Ryan was a respected choice, he was also a narrowly additive choice as he did not bring gender or racial/ethnic diversity to the ticket. In a competitive general election, while running mates rarely make a difference in the electoral outcome, a single state could make the difference between winning and losing the White House. As such, the state from which a running mate hails, as well as key demographic categories, can factor in to the selection decision.

Given the data in Table 8, Clinton—should she become the Democratic nominee in July 2016—might want to consider choosing a Hispanic running mate. Julian Castro, the current Secretary of Housing and Urban Development, the former mayor of San Antonio, Texas, and a rising young star in the Democratic Party has already been mentioned as a possibility in the media. Some believe he could potentially make the state of Texas competitive for Democrats, though this would be a longshot because a Democratic candidate has not won Texas since 1976. Given the likelihood that the Republican nominee will be a man, the nominee may likely consider selecting a woman for the ticket. The positive attention garnered by Carly Fiorina in the Republican primary contests suggests she might be a good choice, although other alternatives exist such as South Carolina Governor Nikki Haley or New Mexico Governor Susana Martinez, both of whom would bring gender and racial/ethnic diversity to the Republican ticket (Haley is of Indian descent while Martinez is Latina).[10]

Notes

1. Jim Thompson, "Six States Signed So Far for 'SEC Primary,' " *Athens Banner-Herald*, October 15, 2015, http://onlineathens.com/election/2015-06-04/six-states-signed-so-far-sec-primary.

2. Adam Nagourney and Jonathan Martin, "Party Rules to Streamline Race May Backfire for G.O.P.," *New York Times*, September 19, 2015, http://www.nytimes.com/2015/09/20/us/new-party-rules-fail-to-speed-up-republican-race.html?_r=0.

3. See "The Official Guide to the 2016 Republican Nominating Process," October 8, 2015, https://www.gop.com/the-official-guide-to-the-2016-republican-nominating-process/.

4. "Democratic Convention Watch," April 5, 2015, http://www.democraticconventionwatch.com/diary/3822/.

5. Henry Olsen, "New RNC Rules Stymie Conservatives in the Primaries," *National Review*, September 3, 2014, http://www.nationalreview.com/article/386913/new-rnc-rules-stymie-

conservativesin-primaries-henry-olsen.

6. "How Iowa Caucus Works," http://2016iowacaucus.com/how-iowa-caucus-works/.

7. Sean McElwee, "The Income Gap at the Polls," *Politico Magazine*, January 7, 2014,

    http://www.politico.com/magazine/story/2015/01/income-gap-at-the-polls-

    113997#ixzz3pxn32CHm.

8. See "Demographics and the 2016 Election Scenarios," RealClearPolitics,

    http://www.realclearpolitics.com/articles/2015/08/26/demographics_and_the_2016_electi

    on_scenarios.html.

9. See "Federal Elections 2012," Federal Election Commission,

    http://www.fec.gov/pubrec/fe2012/federalelections2012.pdf.

10. Lori Cox Han, *In It to Win: Electing Madam President* (New York: Bloomsbury, 2015),

    172–3.

Chapter 4

THE GENERAL ELECTION

Once the party has a nominee, the candidate must then shift gears from the long marathon that was the pre-nomination and nomination phases to the sprint to the finish line that takes place between September and the first Tuesday in November. Candidates must win the popular vote in enough states to amass 270 electoral votes in the Electoral College. During the general election, candidates focus on keeping the voters who were with them during the primary, convincing those who were not on their side to turnout, and attracting voters who did not participate in the nomination phase. Candidates must shift their strategic thinking from the calendar and the rules to defining the narrative of the race and generating appeals to those who are just tuning in to the campaign.

Getting to 270

During the general election phase, everything is magnified, as the two candidates are the center of an enormous amount of attention from both the news media and voters. This is particularly important within the handful of swing states, whose voting outcome and their respective Electoral College votes are not easily predicted. A joint initiative of the American Enterprise Institute, the Brookings Institution, and the Center for American Progress predicts that there will be 11 competitive or so-called battleground states in 2016. They include Colorado, Florida, Iowa, Michigan, Nevada, New Hampshire, North Carolina, Ohio, Pennsylvania, Virginia, and Wisconsin. While there are potential vice presidential candidates from several of these states, the outcome will rely more on generating voter turnout and a successful ground game and organization.[1]

Based on 2008 and 2012, the 2016 race for president will also be the most expensive race in history, particularly with the combination of candidate money, party money, and outside group money. What do candidates do with all this money? The money is primarily spent on television advertising in the battleground states. However, voters in big states with the most Electoral College votes, like California, New York, or Texas, are not likely to see either candidate campaign there nor see numerous television ads. Instead, the bulk of the money, more than $7 billion dollars, used for advertising and campaign organizations, will be focused on those 11 battleground states. Battleground states are so named because the states do not reliably vote for one party over the other. They are in play, meaning that either candidate can win. Turnout matters significantly in the battleground states because the outcome is routinely so close. In 2012, for example, 70 percent of those eligible voted in the battleground state of Colorado. In New York, in contrast, only 53.1 percent of those eligible voted.[2] The fact that Colorado is competitive and gets attention from the candidates and from outside groups clearly spurs citizens to vote. The reverse is also true: lack of attention means only the most motivated participate.

We have become so comfortable with the idea of states consistently voting red or blue that we are ignoring that these reliable voting patterns are based on about half the eligible population participating. What would happen if 30 percent of that 46 percent of New Yorkers who did not vote voted Republican? The state would be red (as in a Republican majority) instead of reliably blue (a Democratic majority). Are there enough voters in the state who would vote for the Republican candidate to turn New York red? We do not know, because they do not participate reliably. What we do know is that an increase in turnout would change the current dynamics where so much time and money is concentrated on a few states. It is another chicken and egg scenario—if more voters voted, candidates would be attentive to those states. But, of course, if more candidates paid attention to those other states, more voters would vote.

Debates

The fight over the CNBC format for the Republican nominating debate in October 2015 reveals how much candidates care about the way they are presented and the way they perform in these live, anything-can-happen televised events. The candidates pushed back against CNBC regarding length (from three hours to two), regarding opening statements (having them), and even during the debate argued with the moderators. For example, Christie yelled at moderators: "Are we really talking about fantasy football? Wait a second, we have $19 trillion in debt, people out of work, ISIS and Al Qaeda attacking us, and we're talking about fantasy football?"

Chris Christie yelling at a CNBC debate (AP Photo/Mark J. Terrill, File)

The debates in the general election are potentially so significant to a candidate's fortunes that the Republican and Democratic parties jointly created the Commission on Presidential Debates in 1987 as a nonpartisan body that would negotiate the format and rules for presidential and vice presidential debates during the general election. In the fall of 2016, there will be four debates, three presidential and one vice presidential. The debates will take place on university campuses in several key states: Wright State University in Dayton, Ohio; Longwood University in Farmville, Virginia; Washington University in St. Louis, Missouri; and the University of Nevada in Las Vegas, Nevada. In addition, according to the Commission, Dominican University of California will "lead an initiative to use technology and social media to engage young voters in a discussion of major issues in the 2016 debates (#DUdebate16)."[3]

Despite the fact that the election has seemingly been running for years by this point, there are voters who have not been paying attention to the race before October 2016. These are citizens who do not affiliate strongly with a political party and who have probably not been interested or active up until this point. They have not donated money nor have they voted in the primary or caucus in their state. Just like the up-for-grabs nature makes the battleground states subject to intense attention from the candidates; the up-for-grabs nature of these voters makes them critical for winning the White House. The debates then serve as an introduction to cues that inattentive voters need to make a selection. Ironically, the debates are fairly meaningless for primary and caucus voters because they already know everything there is to know about their candidate and their opponent. Instead, the debates are opportunities for moments that go viral, such as Romney noting his staff prepared him "binders full of women" when asked about gender diversity within his administration while he served as governor of Massachusetts. He was trying to say he asked his staff to provide him with a pool of qualified candidates who were women in order to make his cabinet more reflective of society. He went on to say some important things about pay equity and having a flexible workplace, but all of that was lost in the viral meme, "binders full of women." There is even a Facebook page called "binders full of women," which has 302,509 likes.[4]

Obama–Romney Debate (AP Photo/Pool-Win McNamee).

The debates can offer the last opportunity for the candidates to shape the narrative used to describe their campaign. Romney thoroughly and surprisingly outperformed Obama in their first debate in October 2012, but the second and third debates provided an opportunity for Obama to remind voters of other storylines about Romney, including his infamous "47 percent" comment to donors: "There are 47 percent of the people who will vote for the president no matter what. All right, there are 47 percent who are with him, who are dependent upon government, who believe that they are victims, who believe the government has a responsibility to care for them, who believe that they are entitled to health care, to food, to housing, to you name it. That's an entitlement." The media firestorm had died a little after his success in the first debate. Having a negative meme go viral after the debate proved to be another hurdle Romney could not surmount. The 2016 nominees will face this same quandary–the need to reach unaffiliated, undecided voters without alienating those already on their side and without saying something that inadvertently derails their bid for the White House.

Notes

1. Ruy Teixeira, William H. Frey, and Robert Griffin, "States of Change: The Demographic Evolution of the American Electorate, 1974–2060," American Enterprise Institute/Brookings Institution/Center for American Progress, February 2015, https://cdn.americanprogress.org/wp-content/uploads/2015/02/SOC-report1.pdf.

2. "2012 November General Election Turnout Rates," United States Election Project, September 3, 2014, http://www.electproject.org/2012g.

3. "CPD Announces Sites and Dates for 2016 General Election Debates," Commission on Presidential Debates, http://www.debates.org/index.php?page=2016debates.

4. Han, *In It to Win,* 146.

Chapter 5

CONCLUSION

As of this writing, it is much too early to accurately predict who will win the White House in November 2016. Following the pre-nomination phase throughout 2015, several viable candidates have emerged in both parties, yet no one is guaranteed to win their party's nomination in what promises to be a fiercely competitive primary battle. With Biden's decision not to enter the Democratic race in October 2015, the 2016 election will be like the 2008 election in that it is an open nomination contest for both parties (meaning that an incumbent president or vice president is not running). The end of a two-term presidency often means that the presidential field for the opposite party will be large and competitive, as is reflected by the Republican field that had 17 initial candidates. The end of the Obama era is also being felt on the Democratic side, as one of the weaknesses of his legacy will be the fact that the Democratic Party has lost strength in numbers of elected officials both at the congressional and state levels on his watch. That has contributed to what many call a shallow bench of candidates on the Democratic side, as there are fewer state governors or prominent members of Congress from which to choose. In addition, Clinton's decision to mount a second presidential campaign after losing the nomination to Obama in 2008 in effect cleared the field of Democratic candidates; her narrative of inevitability (accurate or not) in news media coverage, as well as her skill at fundraising, left little room for establishment Democrats to compete. Yet, perhaps the most prominent storyline of the 2016 election cycle may be the antiestablishment mood of the electorate. Even if establishment candidates win the respective Democratic and Republican nominations, the anger among voters about "politics as usual" in Washington during the early stages of the campaign was felt at many levels.

The ultimate question remains—who will win in November 2016, and will the political environment benefit Democrats or Republicans? History tells us that it is difficult for a political party to win a third term in the White House. This has not occurred since George H. W. Bush won in 1988, though he ended up being a one-term president, losing to Bill Clinton in 1992. Prior to that, the last time one party dominated the White House for more than eight years was during the presidencies of Franklin Roosevelt (1933–1945) and his successor, Harry Truman (1945–1953). This may well work to the benefit of the eventual Republican nominee in 2016.

We also know that voter turnout is crucial. Many factors contributed to Obama's win in 2008, but higher voter turnout was prime among them. Those numbers came from enthusiasm for the candidate (particularly among new voters), and the Obama campaign's successful get-out-the-vote strategy. A less enthused electorate on the Democratic side often leads to Republican victories. If Clinton is the Democratic nominee, she may hold most, but not all, of the so-called Obama coalition, but she will not likely have the record turnout among African American voters, nor is she likely to get the same turnout among young voters. As for women, political science research shows that partisanship, and not gender, is a much stronger factor in how women vote. It is instructive to remember that Romney won among white women and married women in 2012 despite the overall gender gap (which favored Obama at 11 percent). And when looking at the Electoral College map, the so-called blue wall is not impenetrable. With lower voter turnout, and even slightly lower support for Clinton among African American voters in urban areas, some swing states are back in play. Even a slight dip in the numbers among Hispanic voters in states such as Colorado or Nevada could make a difference as well.

The bottom line is that there are many factors still in play as the various phases of the 2016 presidential election continue to unfold, and for all that can be predicted by political scientists, journalists, and other political experts, there are just as many factors that remain unpredictable. Perhaps the only fact that we do know about presidential elections is that, despite all the excitement that surrounds the politics and process, winning the White House does not guarantee that the newly elected president will be successful at governing once he or she takes up residence at 1600 Pennsylvania Avenue.